Swimming with Sea Lions

and Other Adventures
in the Galápagos Islands

by ANN McGOVERN

SCHOLASTIC INC. • *New York*

Library of Congress Cataloging-in-Publication Data

McGovern, Ann.
  Swimming with sea lions and other adventures in the Galápagos
Islands / by Ann McGovern.
   p. cm.
   Summary: In a series of diary entries, a young child describes a
trip to the Galápagos Islands, focusing on the exotic animal life.
   ISBN 0-590-45282-7
   1. Natural history—Galápagos Islands—Juvenile literature.
2. Galápagos Islands—Description and travel—1981—Juvenile
literature. [1. Natural history—Galápagos Islands. 2. Galápagos
Islands—Description and travel.] I. Title.
QH198.G3M39 1992
508.866'5—dc20   91-13130
                                                      CIP
                                                       AC

12 11 10 9 8 7 6 5 4 3 2 1   2 3 4 5 6/9

Printed in the U.S.A.   36

First Scholastic printing, March 1992

Designed by Tracy Halliday

ACKNOWLEDGMENTS

Countless thanks to adventurer-explorer extraordinaire Mike
McDowell of Quark Expeditions who seeks out the best of the
world's wild places and who made my Galápagos adventures possible.

To Quasar Nautica and the enthusiastic, helpful crew of the Mistral.

To naturalist guide Andy Drumm who shared his enlightened
understanding and knowledge of these islands.

To my son Jim Scheiner for his thrilling photograph of the
hammerhead sharks.

To my diving buddy Ruth Petzold who provided the
photographs of "Grandma" and who shared the delightful
surprises of swimming with sea lions and helping me brave
the dangers of wild currents.

To Sasha Muirhead, who loves the giant tortoises, too.

To Eva Moore, my patient, able editor and friend.

Special thanks to my husband, Marty Scheiner, for much more
than his loving encouragement and support. With deepest
admiration, I salute his great courage on this challenging
and rewarding journey and on all journeys to come.

Remembering May Garelick

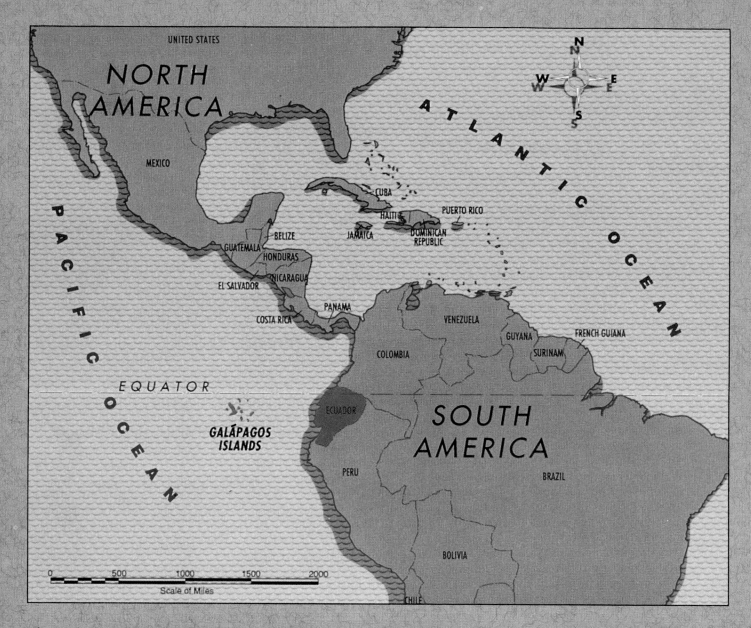

The Galápagos Islands are 600 miles west of the mainland of Ecuador, South America. There are fifteen large islands and about forty small islands. Some of the small ones are just rocks jutting out of the Pacific Ocean.

Day One. First day in the Galápagos!!!! San Cristóbal Island

Dear Diary,

   I can't believe that Grandma and I have already spent almost a whole day in the Galápagos Islands. Everything is like a strange dream.

   Today I walked right up to birds and they didn't fly away! Grandma talked to sea lions — and they talked back with funny barks and burps. I've never seen such tame wild creatures in my whole life!

   Living on a boat is strange, too. Our boat is called the *Mistral*. Grandma and I share a small cabin. There's a tiny bathroom in our cabin. It's funny to think of sleeping and eating and going to the bathroom on a boat for two weeks.

The <u>Mistral</u>—my home for two weeks. There were eight other passengers and four crew members.

The Galápagos has been a dream trip of Grandma's for years. I'm so lucky she asked me to come along.

I think I'll start from the beginning. There was snow on the ground when Grandma and I left New York. After three different plane rides, we came to these hot islands on the equator, in the Pacific Ocean!

When we landed at the little airport, we were met by Andy, our guide. I found out that every boat that travels around the Galápagos Islands has a licensed guide who knows everything about these islands and the creatures who fly, crawl, and swim here.

Grandma is keeping a diary of Andy's facts for me to add to *my* diary. I'm going to put her pages at the end. This is the symbol I'll use to show that there's more information in Grandma's diary.☼

Andy says we'll spend most of our days on shore walking around the islands, looking at the creatures — mostly birds and reptiles.☼ I asked him about swimming, my favorite sport. He said sometimes we'll swim from a beach, and sometimes we'll jump off the boat into the water.

Andy didn't mind when this finch flew up and pulled out a strand of his hair. I never saw anything like that before! Andy said the bird just wanted the hair for its nest.

A few people plan to scuba dive, including Grandma! She says she wants to dive with fish that are found only here. And she wants to look at hammerhead sharks, huge manta rays, and sea turtles.

I was on the ship for only an hour when I saw my first flying fish skimming just above the water.

Still Day One
Later

Dear Diary,
We are anchored close to land. Dozens of sea lions doze and sun on the shore. Others play in the water.

I jumped off the boat and got a big surprise. Even though it's broiling hot in the middle of the day, the waters of the Galápagos Islands feel real cold.

Grandma snorkeled with me. We peered down into the sea through our clear face masks. We use snorkel tubes for breathing, and the fins on our feet make it easy to swim.

Sea lions are everywhere on San Cristóbal Island!

I took this shot of a playful sea lion pup with an underwater camera. Isn't she adorable?

I saw yellow-tailed surgeonfish swimming beneath me -- there must have been a hundred of them!

Suddenly a big body -- then another -- bolted past us. Grandma and I were quickly surrounded by *ten* adorable young sea lions!

It was a circus in the sea! Sea lion pups dived beneath us, blowing silvery bubbles through their noses. They somersaulted and flipped themselves into pretzel shapes. They chased and nipped each other. They are like big kittens. They seemed to be showing off just for us. They never scared me.

But the big male sea lion on shore did scare me with his bellowing roar! The other sea lions answered the bull with barks and coughing and burping sounds. It sounded like they were going to throw up.

Andy told us that the bull sea lions try to keep other males away. They also keep watch for sharks.

Sea lions live on almost every island so I will be seeing a lot of them. I'm glad because so far they are my most favorite creatures.

Still later

Tonight I saw my first Galápagos sunset. The sky was glowing, and the sun was setting over a big rock that rose out of the sea.

My first Galápagos sunset. That big rock is called Kicker Rock because it looks just like a boot.

Grandma and Marty, one of the passengers, are surrounded by giant tortoises on Santa Cruz Island.

Day Two. Santa Cruz

Dear Diary,

This morning we anchored in Academy Bay off Santa Cruz, one of the four islands in the Galápagos where people live.

I'm so excited! After lunch I'm going to see giant Galápagos tortoises –– the largest land tortoises in the world! At the Charles Darwin Research Station I'll get to see them up really close. Grandma says the station was named for Charles Darwin, who sailed to the Galápagos in 1835 on the ship the *Beagle* and later became a famous scientist. ☺

I just found out that *galápagos* means tortoise in old Spanish.

Later

Dear Diary,

I am so mad I could cry!

I read up on giant tortoises before lunch. Once there were hundreds of thousands of these huge tortoises on the Galápagos Islands.

Long ago, explorers, pirates, and seal and whale hunters came here. They stayed at sea for many months, and sometimes years. The fresh meat of the giant tortoises kept them from starving to death. The sailors knew that tortoises can stay alive for a year without food or water, so they stacked them by the hundreds in the damp, dark holds of their ships, one on top of another. Oh, those poor creatures.

Rats are no friends of tortoises, either. There were never rats here until the ships brought them. The rats swam to shore and began to destroy tortoise eggs and young tortoises. Rats are still around today. No wonder there are so few giant tortoises left.

The good news is that today there's hope for the tortoises. Andy told me that thanks to the Charles Darwin Research Station and the National Park Service, a lot of giant tortoises are being saved. ☀

Before bedtime

Dear Diary,

I saw them! I couldn't believe my eyes! I had read that giant tortoises can weigh over 500 pounds so I wasn't expecting a little box turtle. But I never dreamed there could be such big tortoises. And they looked so old with their great wrinkled necks and teary eyes.

At the Research Station the bigger tortoises are kept outdoors in large fenced areas, and the younger ones are in indoor pens.

My favorite tortoise is Lonesome George. Once he lived on Pinta Island with thousands of other tortoises. Hunters came to Pinta and took all the tortoises they could find. But somehow they missed one tortoise.

In 1973, workers from the Darwin Station came to Pinta Island to get rid of the wild goats that were destroying so much of the plants. The workers discovered the one tortoise that was left behind. Since he was the only one of his species left, they named him Lonesome George and brought him back to the station.

This tortoise is hiding in its shell. Maybe I scared it. (I didn't mean to.)

In the middle of the night

Dear Diary,

   I can't stop worrying about tortoises. They're still in danger. Besides the goats that eat the plants and the grasses that are the tortoises' food, there are cats, dogs, pigs, rats, and donkeys that roam the islands and destroy tortoise eggs and baby tortoise hatchlings.

   When I grow up, I want to work at the Charles Darwin Research Station and help save the baby tortoises.

Day Three, Santa Cruz

Spooky <u>scalesia</u> trees grow only in the Galápagos.

Dear Diary,

   What a day! I talked Grandma into letting me go with Andy and a few others to look for giant tortoises in the highlands.
   Andy told me to wear a scarf around my neck, but it was such a hot day that I stuck it in my pocket.
   We got on a rickety old bus and started our climb into the highlands. Pretty soon we were in an evergreen forest. We got out and hiked the rest of the way. The woods smelled good, like spices, but it was spooky. Strange moss hung from the branches of twisted trees.

And talk about mud! Sometimes I was almost up to my knees in muddy goo. We seemed to walk for hours — then I saw my first tortoise in the wild! I was so excited I began to shout.

I guess I shouted too loud because right away its head and feet disappeared into its shell, or *carapace* as Andy calls it. And that carapace was all any of us saw of any tortoise the whole day!

On the way back, I was feeling bad about scaring the tortoise when suddenly I felt a stinging bite on my neck. Then another, and another, till my neck felt like it was on fire!

I began to dance around like crazy. Andy ran over to me and rubbed some cooling lotion on my neck.

He told me I was being bitten by fire ants that drop from trees. If I had worn my scarf around my neck like he had told me to, they wouldn't have been able to attack me.

I squeezed my eyes shut to keep from crying. First, I scared the only tortoise we saw. Second, it was my own stupid fault that I got bitten by fire ants. And third, Andy is mad at me.

Dear Diary, you know what? I'm sorry I ever came to the Galápagos.

Andy's shoes and pants are coated with mud after our hike through the woods. Yuck!

Later

Dear Diary,

Andy's not mad at me after all! He came up on deck of the *Mistral* where I was watching the sunset. Together we watched the sky glow and quickly turn night—black. He told me a story about a special expedition he had gone on to see the giant tortoises on Isabela Island.

With a group of people, he had hiked up to the top of the volcano where everything grows lush green and where the fog swirls so thick and wet that it drips water. The thousands of tortoises that live there aren't shy, like the Santa Cruz tortoises. They didn't even seem to care that people were around. They just kept on munching plants.

When the tents were set up, the tortoises plodded up to inspect them. They sniffed the gear, too, and stepped on it and began to chew on it! The people had to build a fence of logs to keep the curious tortoises out of camp.

Then, Andy said, it started to pour. Dozens of tortoises came to drink the rainwater that collected in pools. Andy said it was magical.

The way he talked, I could picture the whole expedition.

I love Galápagos tortoises more than anything.

A giant tortoise like this can live for over 100 years.

Day Four. Bartolomé Island

Dear Diary,

   Today I had another thrilling surprise. I always thought penguins only live in the coldest lands of the world. Andy says most do. The small Galápagos penguin lives here, on the equator! ☼

   We took a panga ride around Bartolomé Island to see Pinnacle Rock.

This boat, called a <u>panga,</u> takes us from the <u>Mistral</u> to the islands. That's our panga driver, Miguel.

Pinnacle Rock on Bartolomé Island is spectacular!

When we got close to the pinnacle I saw two small penguins standing on a ledge.

As I was taking their picture, I heard a soft kind of moaning, and another penguin came waddling out of the sea, moving by little jumps. It looked around at us and waddled back into the water. It was so cute.

After lunch, Grandma and I grabbed our fins, snorkels, and masks and went snorkeling in the emerald-green water.

I was surprised to see a penguin swimming underwater! It didn't look a bit clumsy. It uses its wings to fly through the water. Penguins can't fly in the air.

Galápagos penguins are the only penguins in the world that live on the equator!

There are lava fields all over the islands. This is a close-up of some lava in a place called Sulivan Bay. The patterns are really neat!

Day Five. Santiago Island

Dear Diary,

   It was weird, hiking across the lava field here. We started early when it was still cool. But then the sun got hotter and hotter, and the lava itself seemed to burn. Sometimes I walked on clinky cinders that sounded like glass breaking. Sometimes I walked on wrinkled, swirly lava. I pretended I was walking on the moon.

   I'm glad I was wearing sneakers. I can't see how Andy can walk on this rocky stuff in sandals. He says he goes barefoot on most of the islands. His feet must be tough!

   On the north end of this island is a bay with a beautiful white sand beach. Behind the beach are two salt lagoons where flamingos live! Andy said we had

A sky full of flamingos.

to be quiet or they would fly away. I crouched behind a bush and held my breath. There must have been about twenty pinky-orangy flamingos, with legs like stilts, long necks, and hooked black bills.

I was being extremely quiet when suddenly I felt this gigantic sneeze coming. I couldn't hold it back. The flamingos took off with a *whoosh*, and I clicked my camera.

Fur seals are smaller than sea lions and have thicker fur.

Later

In the afternoon we visited the fur seal grotto.

Our small panga bobbed wildly up and down in the sea as we landed close to black jagged rocks. It wasn't an easy landing, and I thought some of us might fall in!

But the trip was worth it. We swam and snorkeled with the adorable fur seals for hours. I looked into their huge dark eyes and tried to catch their silver bubbles. They played with us and with each other, making circles and spirals with their graceful bodies.☀

Lava fields, flamingos, and now fur seals — what a wonderful day!

19

Day Six. Tower Island (Genovesa)

Dear Diary,

I could hardly believe what I saw in the bushes today — frigate birds with bright red balloons puffed out under their beaks.

Andy says we're lucky to be here in the spring. It's courtship time, when male frigates inflate their throat pouches into red balloons to attract females.

Grandma pointed to a white-chested bird soaring above us. "That's the female. Watch what happens."

When one of the males in the bushes saw her, he spread his glossy wings wide. His wings began to tremble, and he began a strange-sounding warble. He wagged his beak from side to side, showing off his red pouch. The female flew closer to get a better look.

A male frigate on Tower Island is ready to go courting.

We didn't stick around to see the entire courtship. Andy said it could go on for hours.

Andy says frigates spend most of their lives in the air, feeding and stealing food from other birds. Grandma says they probably even sleep as they fly thousands of miles away from land. I wonder how a bird can sleep while it's flying. I could watch the great frigate birds fly in slow motion for hours, making lazy loops and circles in the sky.

They're not like any other birds in the world!

I love the cute frigate chicks. This one is about three weeks old.

Red-footed boobies in the Galápagos nest in bushes.

Later

Andy showed us some really funny birds with really funny names. They are the red-footed booby and the blue-footed booby. Only in the Galápagos do the red-footed boobies nest in bushes. Their red feet are certainly weird!

Blue-footed boobies are even stranger-looking. Grandma says they look like their webbed feet were dipped in a bucket of blue paint. Their funny waddle makes me laugh.

I love to watch the boobies dive-bomb into the sea. It's truly amazing the way they hurtle down from the sky — sometimes from as high up as eighty feet! They hit the sea, and while they're *under* the water, they catch fish for their dinner.

Blue-footed boobies do a weird courtship dance.

Marine iguanas lose body heat in the water so they sun themselves by the shore, not moving much. They sit on top of each other for warmth.

Day Seven. Fernandina Island

Dear Diary,

I saw dragons today! Dragons with staring eyes, long scaly tails, thin spiny crests running down their backs, and webbed feet with long, sharp claws.

I saw the dragons lying on rocks and crawling on the sand. And wonder of wonders, I saw them coming out of the sea!

I just showed what I wrote to Grandma, who laughed. "It's all true," she said, "but call them by their true name."

OK, here goes. My dragons are marine iguanas or sea lizards. They live only in the Galápagos. And they're the only lizards in the whole entire world who swim and feed in the water.

I got really close to the marine iguanas. I guess I got too close, because one of them spit!

"It's nothing personal," Andy said. Marine iguanas blow salt out of their nostrils. When they're under the water feeding on seaweed or green algae, they take in a lot of salty water.

The divers on board, including Grandma, went diving today to see the iguanas feeding underwater. Marine iguanas almost never have to swim deeper than thirty feet to find seaweed. Grandma was pretty excited about it when she came up from her dive. She said they looked like tiny crocodiles in the water, with their long, sweeping tails.

Grandma called the iguanas beautiful creatures. I don't think I'd like to cuddle up with them, but I guess they are sort of beautiful -- in their own ugly way!

Day Ten. Floreana Island

Dear Diary,

I lost you for two days. I thought maybe a pelican flew away with you, but you were found under some folding chairs. During the time you were lost, I saw some more amazing things, Dear Diary.

Red sally lightfoot crabs look so bright next to the grayish-blackish marine iguanas.

A pelican in a mangrove swamp.

The nuttiest post office in the world is at Post Office Bay on Floreana Island. It's just a blue-and-white barrel, but whalers and sailors used a barrel like this many years ago. You're supposed to drop your postcards and letters into the barrel. I mailed three postcards home, but I wonder if Mom and Dad will ever get them.

Here is what you're supposed to do at Post Office Bay: Take out all the letters and cards from the barrel. Look at the addresses to see if anyone lives in your town. If you find one, take it home with you and either mail it or deliver it in person. Then put your own cards and letters in the barrel and hope that someone else will pick them up and deliver them. ☼

Andy shows me the souvenirs that ships leave at Post Office Bay. I put my mail in the blue-and-white barrel.

Sea turtles come up at night to lay their eggs on Floreana Island. In the morning you can see the tracks.

Later

In the late afternoon, Miguel the panga driver, took us to a long, sandy beach. We saw the tracks that green sea turtles made the night before. This is the time of year that they come out of the water to dig their nests and lay their eggs in the sand. Before going back to the sea, they cover the eggs with sand, using their back flippers as shovels.

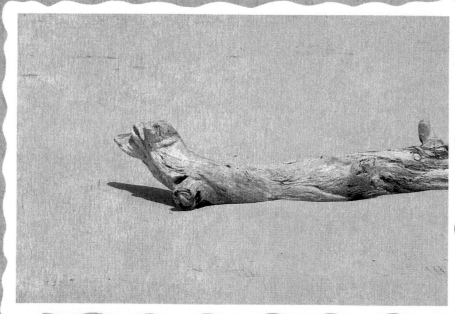

I've seen so many strange creatures that I'm beginning to think even driftwood on the beach is alive!

Later

Dear Diary,

I hope I will always remember the sounds of the Galápagos creatures. Besides the hissing of tortoises and marine iguanas there's the shrill whistle of the male blue-footed booby and the loud honk of his mate. The dismal bellowing of the sea lion bulls and the barks of sea lions answering them. The sighs of the green turtles as they come up to the surface of the sea to breathe. And the weird rattle of the swallow-tailed gulls.

These birds with long red beaks are called oyster catchers. I wonder why?

Water shoots up forty feet through this blowhole.

Day Eleven. Española Island

Dear Diary,

   We landed close to the beach but not close enough! I was up to my knees in water. Lucky I took off my sneakers in the panga or they'd be soaked.

   I think Española is the strangest island of all these strange Galápagos Islands.

   First of all, there's an amazing blowhole. One of the passengers took a cold shower in it! ☼

   For the longest time, I sat at the edge of the cliff, listening to the birds and watching the salt mist blowing over the island.

   There are a ton of birds on Española — chirping finches, Galápagos doves, and bold mockingbirds. One came right up to me to look me over!

A pretty Galápagos dove.

I saw so much on this island. I'd better make a list of everything I remember.

1. blowhole
2. a mixed colony of blue-footed boobies and yet another kind of booby called a *masked booby* (Guess why!)
3. thousands of swallow-tailed gulls
4. lots of sea lions
5. two waved albatrosses
6. lava lizards
7. red and green marine iguanas

There were hundreds of masked boobies on the rim of the cliffs. They looked almost painted, with their bright white feathers and their black face masks and orange eyes. Their webbed feet of olive-green are boring compared to the bright blue and red of the other boobies. But all the booby chicks are adorable.

A masked booby family: mama, poppa, and baby.

Andy wasn't sure the albatrosses would be here yet. Two weeks ago he didn't see one bird. But lucky us! Today we saw two! They are *so* big! ☀

Española is the only island where the marine iguanas are green!

Española Island is also the only place in the world where the waved albatross comes to breed. This one is about to become a mother.

Day Twelve. Santa Fe Island

Dear Diary,

Today I helped rescue a wild creature.

Often, when we go from one island to another, the crew fishes by trolling a long line in the sea. They catch a lot, and we eat a lot of fresh fish.

But today the catch was not a fish at all -- but a bird! A masked booby had dived into the sea to get fish, and it was hooked by the crew's fishing lure. The poor booby was dragged a long way before the crew saw what they had caught!

Pedro, the cook, picked up the booby and turned it upside down. Water poured out of its beak. He set it down on a red towel in the sun.

Look what turned up on the fishing line—
a masked bobby!

When the boat got to Santa Fe Island, I stayed on board while the others went to see a forest of tall cactus trees. I checked up on my bird every ten minutes. I was so worried it might die.

The bird didn't seem to mind me. After a while I stroked its head, and it didn't turn away. And then, after hours of drying out and resting in the sun, the booby fluttered its wings, looked at me for the last time as if to say good—bye, and took off into the sky!

I was never so glad to see a bird fly away in my whole life.

Opuntia cactus trees grow to be thirty feet tall— taller than four tall people standing on each other's shoulders.

Day Thirteen. Plaza Island

Dear Diary,

    Today is our last day. The *Mistral* is anchored in the channel between two islands. Two other boats are here, too.

    On some Galápagos Islands we had the whole place to ourselves. But here there are many tourists! Panga driver Miguel says there are ten times as many people coming to the Galápagos now than fifteen years ago.

    Andy promises that I'll see a new creature today. Am I ready for another new experience? I can hardly keep the old ones straight. That's why you, Dear Diary, are so important, to help remind me of what I saw on what day and where.

There are hundreds of sea lions on Plaza Island.
Grandma made friends with one.

Later

The panga landed right next to a jetty where sea lions lay resting in the sun. When they saw us, they got up and moved. I felt bad about that. It's *their* island, not ours!

But I was glad to see Andy's new creature, Dear Diary. It's another kind of dragon — a land iguana! They are fat, golden-brown dragons with yellow spines, and they don't have webbed toes like the marine iguanas. In front of the tall cactus trees — the *opuntias* — the land iguanas look like tiny dinosaurs.

Today I forgot to remember one important Galápagos rule. Andy reminded me, in a stern voice, that bringing food to any island here is a no-no.

I had stuck a banana in my pants pocket after breakfast and had forgotten all about it. I was sitting on the ground, watching a pretty Galápagos dove, when I remembered the banana and took it out of my pocket to eat. Suddenly an

These guys are in a hurry to get away from our panga.

34

iguana ambled over and began to climb up my leg! I got so excited I stood up fast and startled the poor dragon. It was funny to see that iguana take off. Grandma said it was probably after the banana. There must be something about the color yellow. Iguanas seem to like the yellow blossoms of the prickly pear cactus, too.

The face of the land iguana looks gentle and kind compared to the marine iguana's fierce expression.

The yellow blossoms on the prickly pear cactus attract the land iguana.

On the rocks...
on the beach...
everywhere you look—sea lions looking at you!

Hundreds of sea lions are here. Grandma held her nose and said, "Ah, the sweet stink of sea lions." I *like* the smell. We walked along a sea-lion trail of shiny rocks. Andy says the rocks have been polished by zillions of sea lions that have followed this same trail for hundreds of years.

Sea lions wear sand coats after a roll on the beach

Sea lion bones make the saddest picture.

I saw some white bones of sea lions. But the most horrible sight was a dead iguana. Someone had propped it up to make it look spooky.

I know that all creatures who live must die someday but it makes me sad anyway.

The long white tailfeathers of this red-billed tropic bird stream out like the tail of a kite.

A Galápagos sky just as the sun is setting—a sig[ht] I will never forget.

Still Day Thirteen. Last night on the *Mistral*

Dear Diary,

Tonight's my last sunset. My last dinner on the boat. Today I saw my last sea lions and my last dragon iguanas. Lava gulls hitched their last ride on the panga.

Every day has been so full of surprises.

How can I ever thank Grandma for this wonderful trip?

A sea lion says good-bye to my camera bag.

This is one of the places Grandma dove. It's called "Devil's Crown."

Grandma went on her last dive today. I think she's also sad about the trip ending. Today she saw a sea horse and a manta ray, and she swam with a school of hammerhead sharks! She wasn't even scared!

Grandma and the other scuba divers look happy after a dive.

Grandma took this picture of hammerhead sharks. She says that divers don't have to be afraid of sharks in the Galápagos Islands. There is so much food for them to eat in the waters that they don't need to eat people!

I think my grandma is very brave, anyway. Anyone who dives at a site called "Devil's Crown" has to be brave!

Later, after dinner

We had a special dinner tonight with ice cream and cookies baked in the shape of tortoises. Andy and the crew handed out silly prizes. I got a pencil because I spend so much time writing in my diary. Grandma got a shower cap because she spends so much time underwater. And everyone got a map. Andy marked up the maps, tracing our journey around the islands.

Still later, about nine o'clock

Almost everyone had gone to
their cabins to pack. I was
going over my map with Andy in
the lounge, and Grandma had gone
out on the deck to look at the
Galápagos sky for the last time.
Suddenly I heard her call out,
"Come! Hurry!"

Andy and I raced outside to
the front -- the *bow* -- of the
boat, where Grandma was looking
down into the sea. The sight
made me catch my breath. There
in the black sea, I saw the
silvery outlines of ten big
fish. But it turned out they
weren't fish at all. They were
dolphins. It looked like the
dolphins' bodies were edged in
fire!

Lava gulls seem to like riding on the panga.

I had seen dolphins in the daytime. I loved to watch them playing in the waves, leaping up out of the water, keeping up with the ship.

But I had never seen anything like the night dolphins glowing with stardust. Andy called to everyone to come see. Like me, they were all stunned by the magic of ten silver-edged, fire-lit dolphins swimming below us.

The dolphins gave us their fantastic light show for about twenty minutes. Then ten streaks of light shot across the water -- and the dolphins were gone.

Even though my picture of the dolphins at night didn't come out, I'll always remember them.

I felt I had been given a wonderful gift.
   Good-bye, dolphins! Good-bye to all creatures of the
Galápagos. I'll never forget you.
   Good night, Dear Diary.

MORE ABOUT THE GALÁPAGOS

Here are a lot more facts that Grandma kept for me in her diary.

☀ Day One
The Galápagos Islands, page 6

Most of the islands have two names — a Spanish and an English name. We've used the Spanish names for all of the islands except one. Tower Island is what most people call Genovesa.

☀ Day One
More About Sea Lions, page 9

Sea lions live in groups. One big male bull takes charge of a family of about forty females and their young. Andy says these sea lions are closely related to the California sea lions.

Sea lions sleep or doze on beaches and play in the water. They even ride the waves, like body surfers. Sometimes they swim alongside our panga, leaping high up in the water like dolphins. On white beaches, they look like dark rocks against the water.

☀ Day Two. Santa Cruz
More About Charles Darwin, page 10

Charles Darwin was a young British naturalist whose job on a round-the-world voyage on the *Beagle* was to collect and study plants and animals. In 1835, the *Beagle* stopped at a few Galápagos Islands. Darwin noticed that many of the strange birds and animals were different from one island to the other. Indeed, the islands themselves were different in certain ways. Some had low shrubs and others had tall trees and cactus, due to the different amounts of rainfall.

For over twenty years he thought hard about these differences and finally decided how the creatures might have changed or *evolved*.

For example, when a few tortoises came from the mainland hundreds of thousands of years ago, they may have all looked pretty much the same. But some may have had shells that allowed their necks to stretch just a little higher than the others. On islands where the plants grew tall, these tortoises got more to eat and laid more eggs. Their offspring had slightly higher shells, too. Those that had the highest shells ate most and had the most offspring. So more of each generation of tortoises had higher and higher shells that allowed them to reach much higher to get food. Eventually all of the tortoises on these islands had the higher shells. We call these the *saddleback* tortoises.

On islands where the plants grew low, the tortoises with dome-shaped shells survived the best.

Eventually, fifteen different kinds of tortoises were found on fifteen different islands.

In much the same way, other animals and birds developed in a variety of ways that helped them survive.

Charles Darwin wrote these theories in a book, *On the Origin of Species*, twenty-four years after he visited the Galápagos Islands. People refer to Darwin's theories with the phrase "the survival of the fittest," which means that those species best-suited to their environment are the ones that stay alive.

After Darwin's book was read and talked about, people thought about biology in a different way.

Charles Darwin Research Station, page 11

One hundred years later, in 1959, the Charles Darwin Foundation was formed to protect the unusual life on the Galápagos. Scientists from all over the world come to study the plants and animals.

The Charles Darwin Research Station sends workers to different islands to collect tortoise eggs. They bring the eggs back to the station where they are protected until they hatch. Thousands of hatchlings have been raised at the station. The little tortoises are cared for until they are five years old, old enough to have a good chance of surviving in the wild. Then the tortoises are returned to their own islands where eventually they mate and produce young tortoises.

The creatures of the Galápagos are protected by rules made by the Charles Darwin Research Station and the Galápagos National Park Service.

All the guides make sure the rules are followed. Touching or feeding any of the creatures, wandering off the marked trails, or taking anything -- even a broken shell or a piece of lava -- is against the rules.

Day Four. Bartolomé Island
More About Galápagos Penguins, page 16

It's the Humboldt current that brings in cool water from the Antarctic, making it possible for Galápagos penguins to live here.

Day Five. Santiago Island
How the Galápagos Islands Were Formed, page 18

Millions of years ago, the Galápagos Islands did not exist.

Very deep down in the earth, it was so hot that rocks weren't solid. Instead they were like melted wax. Sometimes this molten rock came to the earth's surface through cracks. It hardened into lava: solid rock. As more lava came out, it piled up into hills. Sometimes the hills grew as tall as the mountains we call volcanos.

If the cracks were beneath the sea, the mountains they formed were sometimes high enough for the tops to stick up above the water. All the islands of the Galápagos are volcanic.

From time to time, an island will erupt

and spew out hot lava. The lava runs down the mountain and forms vast lava fields.

Day Five. Santiago Island
More About Fur Seals, page 19

Once, there were hundreds of thousands of fur seals on the Galápagos Islands. About 150 years ago, hunters killed the seals for their thick fur. Today, with no hunting allowed, the fur seals are making a comeback!

Day Six. Tower Island
More About Frigates, page 21

When the female frigate chooses a mate, she joins her partner in head-wagging. They rub their heads and chests together, and the male surrounds her with his glossy wings.

After they mate, the male frigate's red pouch begins to shrivel up and it loses its bright red color.

Then they go to work building a nest out of sticks. The male snatches twigs from trees, or sometimes from other birds' nests. He even swoops down to pick up branches floating on the water, without getting his wings wet! His mate arranges the sticks into a flimsy platform for the one egg she will lay.

Once the egg is laid, they each take turns sitting on it for fifty-five days and nights! Sometimes one bird is away for a long time while its mate sits quietly on the nest, waiting for up to two weeks without eating or drinking.

At six months, the frigate chick is the same size as its parents. It begins learning to fly, but it will be a long time before it gets good at catching fish far out at sea. It never lands on water; it doesn't have webbed feet.

Frigates can never get their wings wet because their feathers might get waterlogged. They don't have enough oil in their feathers, like true seabirds do.

It must take enormous skill to fly low over the waves and snatch a fish from the water, without getting your wings wet.

More About Boobies, page 22

The female blue-footed booby lays two, sometimes three, eggs. Only the strongest chicks survive.

Blue-footed boobies, unlike the red-footed and the masked booby, hardly ever fly far out to sea. Blue-footed boobies mostly catch fish in the shallow waters around the islands.

Day Seven. Fernandina Island
More About Marine Iguanas, page 24

The female iguana never sees her eggs. After she lays them, she pushes them into a hole. From time to time she sticks her tail into the hole to make sure her eggs are safe. Iguana eggs hatch in about two months.

Day Ten. Floreana Island
More About Post Office Bay, page 25

An old barrel on Floreana Island has been used for mail by passing ships since 1787. The ships heading east dropped mail in the barrel, and the ships heading west took the letters to deliver when they reached their homes.

Day Eleven. Española Island
More About a Blowhole, page 28

A blowhole is made when the surf is forced up into a kind of funnel that forms a hissing, forty-foot fountain.

More About the Waved Albatross, page 30

By April, the waved albatrosses arrive and begin their courtship display — head-circling, sky-pointing, feather-preening, bill-clashing, and noisily calling to each other.

The female albatross lays an enormous white egg right on the ground, not in a nest. When the chick hatches, it's already big! It waddles under shady bushes for protection from the sun while the parents fly off to bring back oily fish. At three months, the chick is as big as an adult bird.

It isn't long before the young are ready to spread their great wings and fly away to the far oceans of the world. But they will return to Española next year.

Day Thirteen. Plaza Island
More About Dolphins at Night, page 42

The light shining from the dolphins' bodies is caused by *bioluminescence* in the water. When the dolphins swim, they disturb the millions of tiny creatures that make up *plankton*. Each tiny creature is bioluminescent and gives off a spark of light, like stardust.